TULIPS

TULIPS

Grange
BOOKS

A QUANTUM BOOK

Published by Grange Books
an imprint of Grange Books Plc
The Grange
Kingsnorth Industrial Estate
Hoo, nr. Rochester
Kent ME3 9ND

ISBN 1-84013-272-8

This book is produced by
Quantum Books Ltd
6 Blundell Street
London N7 9BH

Project Manager: Rebecca Kingsley
Project Editor: Judith Millidge
Design/Editorial: David Manson
Andy McColm, Maggie Manson

The material in this publication previously appeared in
Tulips: An Illustrated Identifier and Guide to Cultivation

QUMSPTP
Set in Futura
Reproduced in Singapore by Eray Scan
Printed in Singapore by Star Standard Industries (Pte) Ltd

Contents

TENDER
TULIPS

The tulip is one of the world's
most popular and widely-grown
flowers, and has been since its
origins in the sixteenth century,
when at the height of the tulip
craze, bulbs changed hands for
vast sums of money. Although
tulip bulbs are now generally
within the budget of any gardener,
their popularity has not waned.
Over the past 50 years there has
been a total revolution in the
types and classes of tulip.

The Origins of Tulips

The well-documented history of the garden tulip starts only in 1554 when bulbs and seeds arrived in western Europe from Turkey. These Turkish tulips were not wild flowers, instead they were highly cultivated products.

TULIPS IN EUROPE

The Belgian diplomat Ogier de Busbecq (1522–1592), envoy of the Holy Roman Emperor to Suleiman the Magnificent, referred to 'tulipam', which had little or no smell but were admired for their beauty and variety of colour. Busbecq sent seeds and bulbs to Vienna. Only five years later in 1559 Conrad Gesner saw tulips in the gardens there. Two years later, they were seen growing in Augsburg and the following year, in 1563, a merchant in Antwerp received a cargo of bulbs from Constantinople. From Flanders the tulip spread throughout Europe.

Left. 'My Lady' – a Darwin hybrid which is a vivid coral orange.

Above. 'Keizerskroon' is one of today's oldest tulips, first cultivated in 1750.

TURKEY AND PERSIA

These early tulips reached the consumer as the end results of experimentation, expertise and experience. The first seedlings from these bulbs comprised all kinds of varieties, early, late and mid-season, and with the colour range known today. Except for minor points of shape and size, modern garden tulips still possess no important characteristics which were not present in the original introduction.

There is every indication that these tulips had been cultivated for centuries, but there is none to say that this took place in Turkey. Suggestions have been made that they originated in Persia where the word for tulip, 'lale', is the same as the Turkish word. Ogier de Busbecq said their name was 'tulipam' in Turkey, however he must have misunderstood the word 'tülbent' for turban being used to describe the shape of the tulip flowers.

Tulips Across the World

Tulips reached England in about 1578. About four years later the Englishman Richard Hakluyt wrote of various flowers named 'tulipas' that were being imported from Austria. The tulip soon became popular in England with a very large number of varieties.

ARRIVAL IN ENGLAND

Then in 1629, John Parkinson, the famous horticulturist wrote his *Paradisus*. He was the first English author to do full justice to the tulip, enumerating 140 varieties: 'they yield us more delight and deserveth true commendation with all lovers of beauty, both for their aspect and admirable colours.'

For a time the fame of the tulip eclipsed that of the rose and the daffodil. Gardener to Charles I, John Tredescant, grew more than 50 varieties, and the taste of the Royal Court was eagerly imitated. Although tulips are not mentioned by Shakespeare or Milton, Herrick refers to them and they were also well-loved by Marvell.

Left. Painted in 1632 at the height of tulipomania, tulips can be seen through the gate in this painting by Rubens.

Above. 'Orange Emperor' and 'Toronto' are both excellent tulips having been grown now for over 30 years.

TULIPOMANINA

The tulip did not reach France, until 1608. However, within a few years, bulbs were exchanged for amazing amounts of money. The craze for spending enormous sums on tulips spread northwards through Flanders to Holland. Here it became a total 'tulipomania'. It was a series of gigantic gambles which ended in national disaster. It was the habit of the tulip, when infected by virus, of breaking into beautiful variegated forms that implemented the gambling.

The prizes if you obtained a winning tulip could be enormous. Tulipo-mania was at its height between 1632 and 1637. During this heady period tulip growing went hand in hand with speculation. In every town in Holland a club for tulip trading was set up, in a chosen tavern. People of every description joined in, mortgaging their homes and estates. It was a dangerous game and many lives were ruined. The bubble finally burst in 1637, when the bottom fell out of the tulip market.

Tulip Popularity Grows

The popularity of the tulip in England, Holland, Flanders and northern France increased rapidly in the eighteenth century. Meanwhile in Turkey something close to a mania developed from 1703, which has developed into a genuine obsessive love of the flower.

EARLY FLEMISH TULIPS

A major change was taking place in Flanders and in the northern cities of France such as Lille. Here a new race of breeder tulips were being grown which were broadly cup-shaped but with a much squarer base. The Flemish and Lille growers were all extremely competent and their bulbs were sold for the highest prices.

MODERN DUTCH TULIPS

The early years of the twentieth century saw a huge expansion in the Dutch tulip bulb industry and it attracted many visitors. Near Lisse, Keukenhof was established in 1949. There bulbs could be shown throughout the season and in greenhouses out of season. Each year enormous crowds attend the Dutch flower festivals.

Left. Industrial bulbfields in the heart of the Dutch tulip bulb region near Lisse, Holland.

Above. Mass colour display of tulips in NCC Gardens in Ottawa, Canada.

TULIPS IN NORTH AMERICA

Tulips have an enormous following in the United States, which can perhaps be attributed in part to the influence of Dutch settlers. There are certainly quite a large number of tulip festivals throughout the country, particularly in those areas where a high proportion of the population is of Dutch origin. Among the best are those held in Holland, Michigan, Pella and Orange City, Iowa; and Albany, New York.

But arguably the greatest North American display of tulips takes place in Canada's capital city, Ottawa. Once again, links with Holland have been influential. After Holland's Queen Juliana gave birth in the Ottawa Civic Hospital, the Dutch began to send tulips to Ottawa every year as a gesture of thanks and goodwill between the countries. A spring festival which is in celebration of the tulip is also held every year in the middle of May.

Classification of Tulips

Tulips have been split into 15 divisions. Divisions 1–11 are known as Garden Tulips, their ancestry is usually not known. Divisions 12–15 are the Botanical Tulips which are either species or hybrids of known species.

1. SINGLE EARLY TULIPS
Cup-shaped single flowers, smaller than the late-flowering varieties. Flowers early to mid April. Height 22–40cm (9–16in).

2. DOUBLE EARLY TULIPS
Fully double flowers which are long-lasting and good for cutting. Flowers mid April. Height 22–40cm (9–16in).

3. TRIUMPH TULIPS
Single large flowers – conical at first and then rounded. Flowers late April to early May. Height 40–50cm (16–20in).

4. DARWIN HYBRID TULIPS
Single large flowers – very large on tall stems. Flowers late April to early May. Height 50–65cm (20–26in).

5. SINGLE LATE TULIPS
Square or oval single flowers – large on tall stems. Flowers early to mid May. Height 60–75cm (24–30in).

6. LILY-FLOWERED TULIPS
Single flowers with distinctive shape and long pointed petals. Flowers early to mid May. Height 50–60cm (20–24in).

7. FRINGED TULIPS
Single flowers with petals that are finely fringed at the edges. Flowers early to mid May. Height 45–60cm (18–24in).

8. VIRIDIFLORA TULIPS
Single flowers with petals that are partially green. Flowers early to late May. Height 30–50cm (12–20in).

CLASSES OF TULIP

EARLIES	1.	Single early	
	2.	Double early	
MID-SEASON	3.	Triumph	
	4.	Darwin hybrid	
LATE SEASON	5.	Single late	
	6.	Lily-flowered	
	7.	Fringed	
	8.	Viridiflora	
	9.	Rembrandt	
	10.	Parrot	
	11.	Double late	
BOTANICAL	12.	Kaufmanniana	
	13.	Fosteriana	
	14.	Greigii	
	15.	Species Tulips	

Note. The coloured icons are used throughout the directory

9. REMBRANDT TULIPS
Square large flowers with feathered, flamed or streaked petals. Flowers early to mid May. Height 45–75cm (18–30in).

10. PARROT TULIPS
Single flowers with deeply frilled and wavy petals. Flowers mid to late May. Height 50–60cm (20–24in).

11. DOUBLE LATE TULIPS
Fully double flowers which are large and long-lasting. Flowers mid to late May. Height 40–60cm (16–24in).

Left. A colourful flowerbed display of Darwin hybrids.

12. KAUFMANNIANA
Low growing hybrids with colourful star-shaped flowers. Flowers early in March. Height 15–25cm (6–10in).

13. FOSTERIANA
Wide and bright flowers often with striped or spotted foliage. Flowers mid April. Height 30–50cm (12–20in).

14. GREIGII
Low growing hybrids that have long-lasting flowers. Flowers April to May. Height 20–35cm (8–14in).

15. SPECIES TULIPS
Mainly dwarf tulips with very small flowers for rockery planting. Flowers March to May. Height 10–25cm (4–10in).

TULIP CLASSES

Key to symbols

CLASS

The flower shape of
each class is shown
(see p.15 for details)

Height
(cm)

BLOOMING PERIOD

PERIOD 1-7

1 March
2 Early April
3 Mid April
4 Late April
5 Early May
6 Mid May
7 Late May

ABBREVIATIONS
FCC First Class Certificate
AM Award of Merit
HC Highly Commended
H Haarlem/Hillegom
W Wisley
RHS Royal Horticultural Society

TULIPA 'IBIS'

'Ibis' is a beautiful deep rose colour shading to silvery white at the edge. The flowers are cup-shaped and are smaller than the later flowering varieties. The flowers open wide in sunny weather.

Classification Single early.
Colour Deep rose with silver edges.
Height 30cm (12in).
Year introduced 1910.
Awards AM W 14.
Flowering period Early to mid April.

30 cm **PERIOD 2-3**

TULIPA 'PRINCE CARNIVAL'

A yellow flamed red bi-coloured tulip, 'Prince Carnival' is recommended for beds, containers and indoors. Strong stemmed, they stand up well in windy and wet weather.

Classification Single early.
Colour Yellow flamed red.
Height 32.5cm (13in).
Year introduced 1930.
Flowering period Early to mid April.

  32.5 cm **PERIOD 2-3**

TULIPA 'KEIZERSKROON'

One of the very oldest tulips in the classified list, being in cultivation since 1750. A good bi-coloured tulip, 'Keizerskroon' is carmine scarlet deeply edged with golden yellow

Classification Single early.
Colour Scarlet edged with yellow.
Height 35cm (14in).
Year introduced 1750.
Flowering period Early to mid April.

35 cm   PERIOD 2-3

TULIPA 'APRICOT BEAUTY'

This tulip was previously classified as a Mendel tulip. Its colour is a delicate shade of soft apricot rose, very faintly tinged with red and with a slightly richer colour in the interior. Not the most robust of tulips, its beauty makes it an essential addition.

Classification Single early.
Colour Soft apricot rose.
Height 40cm (16in).
Year introduced 1953.
Flowering period Early to mid April.

40 cm   PERIOD 2-3

TULIPA 'BESTSELLER'

A sport of 'Apricot Beauty' which has bright coppery orange flowers. Like the parent, 'Bestseller' is not the most robust of tulips and should be given special treatment.

Classification Single early.
Colour Bright coppery orange.
Height 40cm (16in).
Year introduced 1959.
Flowering period Early to mid April.

PRINCESS 'IRENE'

'Irene' is another bi-coloured tulip which is a soft orange with salmon and buff featherings. The blooms are borne on strong stems so they stand up well in rainy and windy weather.

Classification Single early.
Colour Soft orange with salmon.
Height 32.5cm (13in).
Year introduced 1949.
Flowering period Early to mid April.

TULIPA 'PEACH BLOSSOM'

This is a sport of the tulip 'Murillo'. The flowers are fully double and are long-lasting. The stems are sturdy but slightly shorter than the single earlies.

Classification Double early.
Colour Bright pink.
Height 25cm (10in).
Year introduced 1890.
Awards AM H 13.
Flowering period Mid April.

TULIPA 'ORANGE NASSAU'

The flowers of this tulip are good for cutting. They open wide, and are a popular choice for containers, window boxes and for forcing indoors.

Classification Double early.
Colour Deep orange flushed red.
Height 25cm (10in).
Year introduced 1930.
Flowering period Mid April.

TULIPA 'SCARLET CARDINAL'

Considered to be the best of the double earlies, 'Scarlet Cardinal' is a vivid tulip, bright scarlet shaded orange, and of a similar stature to the 'Murillos'. It has a forcing time of 10 December.

Classification Double early.
Colour Bright scarlet.
Height 25cm (10in).
Year introduced 1914.
Awards AM H 15.
Flowering period Mid April.

TULIPA 'BABY DOLL'

One of the smallest of the 'Murillo' group of sports, 'Baby Doll' is a deep buttercup yellow, The flowers are long-lasting, but the multi-petalled blooms may bend over after heavy rain, despite being shorter than the Single Earlies.

Classification Double early.
Colour Deep buttercup yellow.
Height 20cm (8in).
Year introduced 1961.
Flowering period Mid April.

TULIPA 'ATTILA'

Triumph tulips were introduced following the First World War and are a cross between a May-flowering tulip and a single early. They have single flowers. 'Attila' is a light purple variety.

Classification Triumph tulips.
Colour Light purple violet.
Height 50cm (20in).
Year introduced 1945.
Flowering period Late April to early May.

| | 50 cm | PERIOD 4-5 |

TULIPA 'ARABIAN MYSTERY'

The flowers of this Triumph tulip are a deep purple violet, edged in white. The single flowers are conical at first, then rounded. They are suitable for exposed sites as the stems are sturdy.

Classification Triumph tulips.
Colour Deep purple violet edged in white.
Height 45cm (18in).
Year introduced 1953.
Flowering period Late April to early May.

| | 45 cm | PERIOD 4-5 |

TULIPA 'DREAMING MAID'

'Dreaming Marvel' is a robust tulip
which can be grown in light shade.
They are suitable for beds and borders
which will have to be cleared for
summer bedding.

Classification Triumph tulips.
Colour Violet edged in white.
Height 50cm (20in).
Year introduced 1934.
Flowering period Late April to early
May.

TULIPA 'HIBERNIA'

A robust white tulip, 'Hibernia' has
single flowers and is reasonably vigorous.
They give an excellent show towards the
end of April.

Classification Triumph tulips.
Colour White.
Height 47.5cm (19in).
Year introduced 1946.
Flowering period Late April to early
May.

TULIPA 'MERRY WIDOW'

'Merry Widow' is a spectacular
bi-colour tulip, magenta red with white
edges. The stems are robust and able
to withstand planting in exposed sites.

Classification Triumph tulips.
Colour White edged magenta.
Height 32.5cm (13in).
Year introduced 1942.
Awards AM H 43.
Flowering period Late April to early
May.

TULIPA 'KEES NELIS'

'Kees Nelis' has large flowers but not as
big as the Darwin Hybrids. It can be
grown in beds and borders, even in light
shade. This is a good example of a
red-edged yellow.

Classification Triumph tulips.
Colour Red-edged yellow.
Height 37.5cm (15in).
Year introduced 1951.
Flowering period Late April to early
May.

TRIUMPH

TULIPA 'VALENTINE'

'Valentine' is another superb bi-coloured tulip, rose-pink with a hint of purple, edged in white. An extremely robust tulip with single flowers, and sturdy stems, they make excellent flowers for bouquets.

Classification Triumph tulips.
Colour Rose pink edged white.
Height 50cm (20in).
Year introduced 1970.
Flowering period Late April to early May.

 50 cm PERIOD 4-5

TULIPA 'ABU HASSAN'

The colouring of this tulip is somewhat unusual – a glowing cardinal red with chrysanthemum stripes on a small buttercup yellow edge. They can be a vigorous tulip and give an excellent show.

Classification Triumph tulips.
Colour Cardinal red with buttercup yellow edges.
Height 50cm (20in).
Year introduced 1976.
Flowering period Late April to early May.

  50 cm PERIOD 4-5

TULIPA 'ORANGE SUN'

This was the first non-red Darwin hybrid, introduced in 1947, sometimes called 'Oranjezon'. Originally classified as a Triumph tulip, it was not transferred to the Darwin section until many years later. Blooms later than most of the other Darwin tulips.

Classification Darwin hybrid.
Colour Pure orange.
Height 55cm (22in).
Year introduced 1947.
Awards AM H 64.
Flowering period Late April to early May.

 55 cm · PERIOD 4-5

TULIPA 'BIG CHIEF'

A large tulip, 'Big Chief' is a very good bedding variety, but will not take kindly to to being left in the ground or naturalised. The flowers are rose madder, edged orange-red with a flush of orange on the inside.

Classification Darwin hybrid.
Colour Rose with orange-red.
Height 65cm (26in).
Year introduced 1959.
Awards FCC W 69 AM H 60.
Flowering period Late April to early May.

 65 cm · PERIOD 4-5

DARWIN HYBRIDS

TULIPA 'OXFORD'

'Oxford' is a favourite red tulip which can, when lifted, produce an excellent new bulb for next year's flowering together with a reasonable number of offsets. The blooms are rounded and appear on tall stems.

Classification Darwin hybrid.
Colour Scarlet.
Height 60cm (24in).
Year introduced 1945.
Awards FCC W 78 AM H 53.
Flowering period Late April to early May.

TULIPA 'GOLDEN SPRINGTIME'

A sport of red Darwin tulips, 'Golden Springtime' is a lovely yellow colour. The flowers are large on long stems and appear earlier than the ordinary Darwins.

Classification Darwin hybrid.
Colour Yellow.
Height 60cm (24in).
Year introduced 1945.
Awards FCC W 78 AM H 53.
Flowering period Late April to early May.

TULIPA 'DAWNGLOW'

An excellent hybrid, 'Dawnglow' is a sport of 'Red Matador' and has the most beautiful combination of colours. A pale apricot flushed with carmine with a hint of orange on the interior. This tulip needs to be planted early to give a good show.

Classification Darwin hybrid.
Colour Apricot flushed with carmine.
Height 60cm (24in).
Year introduced 1965.
Flowering period Late April to early May.

TULIPA 'PINK IMPRESSION'

Considered to be the best pink of all, 'Pink Impression' was produced in 1979. On the outside it is veined empire rose with neyron rose flame and a red feathered edge. On the inside it is a bright claret rose with a black base and small yellow edge.

Classification Darwin hybrid.
Colour Rose with a red feathered edge.
Height 60cm (24in).
Year introduced 1979.
Flowering period Late April to early May.

DARWIN HYBRIDS

TULIPA 'IVORY FLORADALE'

There are no Darwin hybrid whites in
this section but this tulip is the nearest.
The colour is an ivory yellow on the
outside and creamy yellow on the inside,
possibly spotted with carmine red.

Classification Darwin hybrid.
Colour Ivory yellow.
Height 60cm (24in).
Year introduced 1965.
Flowering period Late April to early
May.

60 cm · PERIOD 4-5

TULIPA 'OLYMPIC FLAME'

A sport of 'Olympic Gold', this tulip is
a mimosa yellow flamed deep red. The
blooms are single, large and usually
rounded. 'Olympic Flame' is a tall tulip
with a long stem.

Classification Darwin hybrid.
Colour Yellow flamed deep red.
Height 52.5cm (21in).
Year introduced 1971.
Flowering period Late April to early
May.

52.5 cm · PERIOD 4-5

TULIPA 'ARISTOCRAT'

'Aristocrat' is a popular tulip for borders and around shrubs, it is a clear magenta pink with a light edge and very large flowers. They make good cut flowers.

Classification Single late.
Colour Magenta pink with a light edge.
Height 60cm (24in).
Year introduced 1935.
Awards AM H 38.
Flowering period Early to mid May.

60 cm

PERIOD 5-6

TULIPA 'ROSY WINGS'

The flowers of this tulip are a very distinct shape, almost lily flowering. The flowers are very long and a radiant pink colour. They are good for providing colour after the early varieties have faded.

Classification Single late.
Colour Radiant pink.
Height 57.5cm (23in).
Year introduced 1944.
Awards AM H 47.
Flowering period Early to mid May.

57.5 cm

PERIOD 5-6

TULIPA 'HALCRO'

These tulips are robust, tall and vigorous
and were introduced by the Segers
Brothers. The colour is a deep salmon
carmine with a yellow base and a large
oval-shaped flower.

Classification Single late.
Colour Salmon carmine with a
yellow base.
Height 70cm (28in).
Year introduced 1949.
Awards FCC H 64 AM W 77.
Flowering period Early to mid May.

TULIPA 'RENOWN'

Another tall and robust introduction by
the Segers Brothers, this time a light
carmine red with a yellow base. The
flowers are large and oval-shaped.

Classification Single late.
Colour Carmine red with yellow.
Height 65cm (26in).
Year introduced 1965.
Awards FCC H 51 AM W 68.
Flowering period Early to mid May.

TULIPA 'LANDSEADLE'S SUPREME'

'Landseadle's Supreme' is a long lasting tulip. An excellent cherry red on strong stems, it is useful in borders and beds. The straight stems are stout and make good cut flowers.

Classification Single late.
Colour Cherry red.
Height 65cm (26in).
Year introduced 1958.
Awards FCC H 61 FCC W 77.
Flowering period Early to mid May.

 65 cm PERIOD 5-6

TULIPA 'SHIRLEY'

'Shirley' is a white tulip with a narrow edge of soft purplish blue, lightly spotted with the same colour. The height of these tulips lends them elegance and they add an old-fashioned charm to a garden.

Classification Single late.
Colour White with purplish blue spots.
Height 60cm (24in).
Year introduced 1963.
Flowering period Early to mid May.

 60 cm PERIOD 5-6

TULIPA 'PANDION'

A bi-colour tulip with large flowers which are purple edged in white, 'Pandion's' stiff, erect stems are strong enough to resist all but the harshest of spring weather.

Classification Single late.
Colour Purple edged in white.
Height 60cm (24in).
Year introduced 1965.
Awards FCC H 54 AM W 57.
Flowering period Early to mid May.

TULIPA 'DILLENBURG'

A tulip with an interesting colour combination of orange terracotta. 'Dillenburg' is one of the latest flowering tulips. It is a plant that will prolong the colourful show of any garden even further.

Classification Single late.
Colour Orange terracotta.
Height 65cm (26in).
Year introduced 1916.
Awards FCC H 37.
Flowering period Early to May.

TULIPA 'MARIETTE'

'Mariette' is a tall variety of tulip with long pointed petals, reflexed at the tips. The shape and colour are very distinctive and elegant and make it very suitable for flower arranging.

Classification Lily-flowered.
Colour Deep satin rose with a white base.
Height 60cm (24in).
Year introduced 1942.
Awards FCC H 50 AM W 68.
Flowering period Early to mid May.

60 cm

PERIOD 5-6

TULIPA 'MARJOLEIN'

A striking tulip which is orange and carmine rose with pepper red inside, 'Marjolein's ' strong stems are ideal for formal bedding and flower arranging.

Classification Lily-flowered.
Colour Orange and carmine rose.
Height 57.5cm (23in).
Year introduced 1962.
Awards AM W 82.
Flowering period Early to mid May.

57.5 cm

PERIOD 5-6

TULIPA 'CHINA PINK'

This tulip has beautiful deep pink flowers which are an exquisite rose-pink within. Considered to be a good example, 'China pink' has satin pink coloured petals which arch outward and are slightly pointed.

Classification Lily-flowered.
Colour Satin pink.
Height 50cm (22in).
Year introduced 1944.
Flowering period Early to mid May.

50 cm

TULIPA 'MAYTIME'

This lily-flowered tulip is a purple violet with white edging. The stems are strong and they are useful for formal borders and flower arranging. The resemblance of the flowers to lilies is marked in this variety.

Classification Lily-flowered.
Colour White-edged purple violet.
Height 47.5cm (19in).
Year introduced 1962.
Flowering period Early to mid May.

47.5 cm

TULIPA 'BALLADE'

'Ballade' has waisted flowers and long,
pointed petals that arch gracefully out-
wards at the tips. The blooms have long
pointed petals and are a deep mauve
colour, edged in contrasting white.

Classification Lily-flowered.
Colour White-edged violet mauve.
Height 47.5cm (19in).
Year introduced 1953.
Flowering period Early to mid May.

TULIPA 'ALADDIN'

This elegant tulip has robust stems,
bold, greyish leaves and is weather
resistant. The leaves contrast well
against the crimson pointed petals with
a yellow edge.

Classification Lily-flowered.
Colour Crimson with a yellow edge.
Height 50cm (20in).
Year introduced 1942.
Flowering period Early to mid May.

TULIPA 'BELLFLOWER'

Often planted as a focal point in gardens, these tulips have delicately fringed edges. The flowers are single and rose bengal outside and cherry red inside.

Classification Fringed.
Colour Pink.
Height 50cm (20in).
Year introduced 1970.
Flowering period Early to mid May.

TULIPA 'BURGUNDY LACE'

These are showy, vigorous plants with a crystalline fringe to their wine red petals. For most of its life, it has been one of the cheapest tulips in the fringed group of tulips.

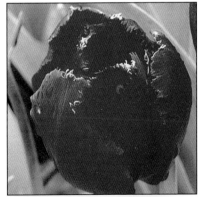

Classification Fringed.
Colour Wine red.
Height 65cm (26in).
Year introduced 1961.
Awards AM W 70.
Flowering period Early to mid May.

TULIPA 'FANCY FRILLS'

A popular new variety of tulip, the exterior of 'Fancy Frills' is ivory white. The top and side of the petals are edged with rose bengal and a crystalline white rose-coloured fringe.

Classification Fringed.
Colour Rose with white base.
Height 50cm (20in).
Year introduced 1972.
Flowering period Early to mid May.

50 cm

PERIOD 5-6

TULIPA 'FRINGED ELEGANCE'

This hybrid tulip is a sport of 'Jewel of Spring' and was introduced by the Segers Brothers. They have long stems and bear enormous, brightly coloured flowers.

Classification Fringed.
Colour Creamy yellow.
Height 60cm (24in).
Year introduced 1974.
Awards AM W 74.
Flowering period Early to mid May.

60 cm

PERIOD 5-6

FRINGED TULIPS

TULIPA 'ARTIST'

'Artist' is a dwarf variety of tulip with distinctive green stripes or blotches. The interior is salmon rose and green, outside it is purple and salmon rose. It grows to a height of 28cm (11in).

Classification Viridiflora.
Colour Salmon and green.
Height 28cm (11in).
Year introduced 1947.
Awards AM W 47.
Flowering period Early to late May.

28 cm

PERIOD 5-7

TULIPA 'GREENLAND'

One of the first hybrids from *Tulipa viridiflora* with stiff stems, and a striking rose-edged green colour. They are grown mainly for cutting as their unusual markings make them a novelty.

Classification Viridiflora.
Colour Rose-edged green.
Height 50cm (20in).
Year introduced 1955.
Awards AM W 60.
Flowering period Early to late May.

50 cm

PERIOD 5-7

TULIPA 'COURT LADY'

These tulips make an excellent show in the border, with their green and white colouring. They are mostly used for flower arranging as they have strong stems and distinctive flower characteristics

Classification Viridiflora.
Colour Green and white.
Height 40cm (16in).
Year introduced 1956.
Flowering period Early to late May.

TULIPA 'SPRING GREEN'

Of the newer varieties, this tulip is the cheapest and probably one of the most vigorous. They have a neat head of orchid green with a broad white edge. The inside of the flower is orchid yellow shading to ivory white at the tips.

Classification Viridiflora.
Colour Orchid green with white edge.
Height 40cm (16in).
Year introduced 1969.
Flowering period Early to late May.

TULIPA 'CORDELL HULL'

Many suggest that Rembrandt tulips are now obsolete because their unusual markings were originally caused by a virus. 'Cordell Hull' is an example of a virus-free modern tulip.

Classification Rembrandt.
Colour Red with white feathered edges.
Height 45–75cm (18–30in).
Flowering period Early to mid May.

TULIPA 'SAN MARINO'

These tulips, with their striking flamed petals, are another example of a virus-free Rembrandt. The dense red beams of colour run up the centre of the bright yellow petals.

Classification Rembrandt.
Colour Yellow with red flames.
Height 45–75cm (18–30in).
Flowering period Early to mid May.

TULIPA 'BLUE PARROT'

The appearance of these tulips is spectacular with cut and twisted petals, giving them an exotic appearance. They are sensitive to poor weather and should be planted in a protected spot.

Classification Parrot.
Colour Violet.
Height 60cm (24in).
Year introduced 1935.
Awards AM H 35.
Flowering period Mid to late May.

60 cm

PERIOD 6-7

TULIPA 'ESTELLA RIJNVELD'

A sport of 'Red Champion' this tulip has waved petals of white richly marked raspberry red. The deeply feathered petals are very characteristic and distinctive.

Classification Parrot.
Colour White with raspberry red.
Height 60cm (24in).
Year introduced 1954.
Flowering period Mid to late May.

60 cm

PERIOD 6-7

TULIPA 'TEXAS GOLD'

This tulip is a sport of 'Inglescombe Yellow' and is a clear yellow with a narrow red ribbon round the edges of the petals. 'Texas Gold' has three more sports 'Texas Cocktail', 'Texas Fire' and 'Texas Flame'.

Classification Parrot.
Colour Yellow with red feathering.
Height 52.5cm (21in).
Year introduced 1944.
Flowering period Mid to late May.

TULIPA 'FLAMING PARROT'

A sport of 'Red Parrot', this variety of tulip has flowers of a creamy yellow flamed and feathered rosy red. 'Flaming Parrot' is a most spectacular tulip with an eye-catching exotic appearance in any flower arrangement.

Classification Parrot.
Colour Creamy yellow with red.
Height 60cm (24in).
Year introduced 1968.
Flowering period Mid to late May.

TULIPA 'MOUNT TACOMA'

This tulip has large, long-lasting flowers but is not as popular as the tulips in the Double Earlies group. The blooms are filled with petals and are sometimes referred to as peony-flowered tulips.

Classification Double late.
Colour White.
Height 55cm (22in).
Year introduced 1926.
Awards FCC H 39.
Flowering period Mid to late May.

  55 cm PERIOD 6-7

TULIPA 'ALLEGRETTO'

The blooms are cup-shaped on this tulip but, are so large that, they are too heavy for the stems. To prevent them toppling over, plant the bulbs closely together in a sheltered spot. Some support may also be needed.

Classification Double late.
Colour Yellow-edged red.
Height 35cm (14in).
Year introduced 1963.
Flowering period Mid to late May.

  35 cm PERIOD 6-7

TULIPA 'LILAC PERFECTION'

'Lilac Perfection' is considered to be one of the best lilacs in this section. With fully double flowers, these tulips have flower heads which resemble those of peonies.

Classification Double late.
Colour Deep rose.
Height 50cm (20in).
Year introduced 1910.
Awards AM H 39.
Flowering period Mid to late May.

TULIPA 'UNCLE TOM'

'Uncle Tom' is an eyecatching tulip with peony styled flowers. The flowers are a maroon red and so large that they can be badly damaged by rain and strong wind if not protected.

Classification Double late.
Colour Maroon red.
Height 30cm (20in).
Awards AM H 39.
Flowering period Mid to late May.

TULIPA 'MAY WONDER'

'May Wonder' is a typical example of a double late tulip, with its large multi-petalled head. It is a deep rose colour and needs protection from wind and rain.

Classification Double late.
Colour Rose.
Height 40cm (16in).
Year introduced 1951.
Flowering period Mid to late May.

  40 cm PERIOD 6-7

TULIPA 'ANGELIQUE'

'Angelique' is one of the most beautiful tulips in this section and extremely popular, even though it has been in cultivation for over 30 years. The colour is a pale pink with a lighter edge.

Classification Double late.
Colour Pale pink.
Height 30cm (12in).
Year introduced 1910.
Awards AM W 14.
Flowering period Mid to late May.

  30 cm PERIOD 6-7

TULIPA 'THE FIRST'

This tulip is usually the first to bloom in
this group, being brighter and larger
than the species and just as vigorous.
The long, wide, star-shaped flowers
are red and white.

Classification Kaufmanniana.
Colour Red and white.
Height 25cm (10in).
Year introduced 1910.
Flowering period March.

TULIPA 'EARLY HARVEST'

'Early Harvest' is one of the most free-
flowering tulips and gives off many
offsets. It is a reddish orange tulip with
a yellow edge and the inside is orange
flamed on yellow.

Classification Kaufmanniana.
Colour Reddish orange with yellow
edge.
Height 20cm (8in).
Year introduced 1966.
Awards AM H 73.
Flowering period March.

48

TULIPA 'LOVE SONG'

Similar to 'Early Harvest', but the exterior is somewhat redder and the yellow edge is narrower. A low growing variety they are ideal for the rockery, containers and for naturalising in grass.

Classification Kaufmanniana.
Colour Reddish orange with yellow.
Height 20cm (8in).
Year introduced 1966.
Flowering period March.

TULIPA 'SHOW WINNER'

The best of the early reds, 'Show Winner' is also vigorous and robust. Their compactness makes them good plants for rock gardens where they can grow in small groups.

Classification Kaufmanniana.
Colour Bright scarlet.
Height 15–25cm (6–8in).
Year introduced 1966.
Flowering period March.

KAUFMANNIANA

49

TULIPA 'CESAR FRANCK'

This is usually the earliest of this group. It is a carmine red and gold and has green leaves. The flowers open into colourful stars in full sunlight which makes them a good choice for border edges and rock gardens

Classification Kaufmanniana.
Colour Carmine red and gold.
Height 30cm (12in).
Year introduced 1940.
Flowering period March.

30 cm

PERIOD 1

TULIPA 'DUPLOSA'

'Duplosa' is a very attractive form which is very different from the species. It is uniquely semi-double in raspberry pink with a gold centre. It is sometimes the first to bloom in the garden.

Classification Kaufmanniana.
Colour Raspberry pink.
Height 22.5cm (9in).
Year introduced 1955.
Flowering period March.

22.5 cm

PERIOD 1

TULIPA 'CORONA'

This tulip has the best centre in the kaufmanniana section, apart from 'Joseph Kafka', it is gold with a broad scarlet band. The petals are red and pale yellow.

Classification Kaufmanniana.
Colour Red and pale yellow.
Height 25cm (10in).
Year introduced c.1943.
Awards AM W 48.
Flowering period March.

TULIPA 'BERLIOZ'

'Berlioz' is a very bright and cheerful tulip. There are red blotches on the outside but it is often described as being all-gold, due to the appearance it gives when fully open.

Classification Kaufmanniana.
Colour Gold with red blotches.
Height 20cm (8in).
Year introduced 1942.
Awards AM W 39.
Flowering period March.

TULIPA 'SPRING PEARL'

The stems of this tall hybrid tulip are prone to damage by strong winds. The flowers are large, a pearl grey colour edged deep pink, inside they are pink with a yellow base.

Classification Fosteriana.
Colour Pearl grey edged deep pink.
Height 45cm (18in).
Year introduced 1955.
Flowering period April.

  45 cm PERIOD 2-4

TULIPA 'ORANGE EMPEROR'

'Orange Emperor' is an outstanding tulip with stronger stems than others and can be grown virtually anywhere. The flowers are a carrot orange with a buttercup centre. They have remarkably wide flowers and the foliage is often striped or spotted.

Classification Fosteriana.
Colour Carrot orange.
Height 50cm (20in).
Year introduced 1962.
Flowering period April.

 50 cm PERIOD 2-4

TULIPA 'PURISSIMA'

Another outstanding tall tulip, 'Purissima' is often described as the best white tulip ever raised. Sometimes called 'White Emperor', it is a milky white colour with a yellow centre. The excellent shape and stature help it to stand up to almost any weather.

Classification Fosteriana.
Colour Milky white.
Height 50cm (20in).
Year introduced 1943.
Awards AM H 49.
Flowering period April.

TULIPA 'SWEETHEART'

This is a sport of 'Purissima', with barium yellow towards the bottom of the bloom and ivory white at the top. It is an attractive tulip and has become very popular since its introduction in 1976.

Classification Fosteriana.
Colour Yellow and white.
Height 37.5cm (15in).
Year introduced 1976.
Flowering period April.

TULIPA 'CANTATA'

'Cantata' is one of the shorter stemmed fosterianas which is considered the best of the group. It is a vivid orange scarlet with a faint buff flush up the middle of the petals, which bloom above glossy apple-green foliage.

Classification Fosteriana.
Colour Vivid orange scarlet.
Height 27.5cm (11in).
Awards AM H 42.
Flowering period April.

TULIPA 'SALUT'

One of the shorter fosterianas in the group, 'Salut' is sulphur white edged with carmine pink, with a black yellow edged base. Robust and vigorous, they are very easy to grow.

Classification Fosteriana.
Colour Sulphur white with carmine pink.
Height 25cm (10in).
Year introduced 1955.
Flowering period April.

TULIPA 'RONDO'

A bi-colour similar to 'Reginald Dixon'. 'Rondo' has a scarlet edged gold exterior, inside there is a golden centre blotched red. Fosteriana tulips are sometimes referred to as 'Emperor' tulips.

Classification Fosteriana.
Colour Gold with scarlet streaks.
Height 40cm (16in).
Year introduced 1952.
Flowering period April.

  40 cm **PERIOD 2-4**

TULIPA 'TOULON'

One of a number of hybrids with greigii leaves, 'Toulon' is the result of cross-breeding. It is slightly short with good stems. It is a vivid deep orange tulip with a centre that is a deep brown edged yellow with pale yellow anthers. The leaves are beautifully striped a reddish brown.

Classification Fosteriana.
Colour Orange with brown centre.
Height 37.5cm (15in).
Year introduced 1943.
Awards AM H 49.
Flowering period April.

  37.5 cm **PERIOD 2-4**

TULIPA 'TORONTO'

Although some greigii dislike heavy soil and are prone to slug attack, this particular tulip is vigorous in any soil. It can be either multi-flowering, branch flowering or bunch flowering. An extremely good bulb maker which recently has been shown to throw sports.

Classification Greigii.
Colour Coral pink with a yellow base and brown blotches.
Height 30cm (12in).
Year introduced 1963.
Flowering period April to May.

TULIPA 'DREAMBOAT'

This is a large-flowered dwarf tulip which is a yellow flamed red, giving the impression of pink colouring on these long-lasting flowers. The foliage is an unusual brown-marbled colour.

Classification Greigii.
Colour Yellow flamed red.
Height 25cm (10in).
Year introduced 1953.
Awards AM W 66.
Flowering period April to May.

TULIPA 'ORATORIO'

'Oratorio' is an apricot rose colour with a black base and extremely attractive brown-marbled foliage. This is a large-flowered dwarf species.

Classification Greigii.
Colour Apricot rose and a black base.
Height 17.5cm (7in).
Year introduced 1952.
Awards AM H 49.
Flowering period April to May.

17.5 cm

PERIOD 2-7

TULIPA 'ROSEANNA'

A bi-colour greigii, 'Roseanna' opens red and white and flowers off-pink. Inside, the centre is yellow with a red ring and brownish blotches and also flowers of pink.

Classification Greigii.
Colour Red and white with pink.
Height 40cm (16in).
Year introduced 1952.
Flowering period April to May.

40 cm

PERIOD 2-7

G R E I G I I

TULIPA 'DONNA BELLA'

This is a dwarf cultivar with exceptional foliage of a green and purple pattern on the upperside. The flowers are flushed purple on the exterior.

Classification Greigii.
Colour Creamy yellow flushed purple.
Height 20cm (8in).
Year introduced 1955.
Flowering period April to May.

20 cm

PERIOD 2-7

TULIPA 'PLAISIR'

'Plaisir' is a good bi-colour which is a very good grower. The blooms are red edged sulphur both inside and out with a black and yellow base.

Classification Greigii.
Colour Red edged sulphur.
Height 22.5cm (9in).
Year introduced 1953.
Flowering period April to May.

22.5 cm

PERIOD 2-7

TULIPA PULCHELLA HUMILIS

Until recently, this was simply called
T. humilis. The common form is coloured
a deep violet pink with a yellow centre.
These are dwarf tulips suitable for
permanent planting in rockeries.

Classification Species tulips.
Colour Violet pink with yellow centre.
Height 10cm (4in).
Year introduced 1982.
Flowering period March.

TULIPA PULCHELLA VIOLACEA

Another dwarf tulip similar in everyway
to *T. humilis pulchella,* in all but the
base which in this tulip is black. Plant
in rockeries or borders where it can be
left permanently.

Classification Species tulips.
Colour Magenta rose with a black
base.
Height 10cm (4in).
Flowering period March.

SPECIES TULIPS

TULIPA BIFLORA

A multi-flowering species with very small white flowers, with a hint of green and a yellow centre. This tulip originates from Russia and can bear up to five blooms per stem. It needs uplifting and replanting annually or it soon dies out.

Classification Species tulips.
Colour White with a hint of green.
Height 17.5cm (7in).
Flowering period March.

TULIPA URUMIENSIS

A dwarf multi-flowering species with small flowers which comes from N.W. Iran. Similar in appearance to *T. tarda*, this tulip is olive-red without and entirely buttercup-yellow within.

Classification Species tulips.
Colour Clear yellow.
Height 12.5cm (5in).
Year introduced c.1932.
Awards FCC W 70.
Flowering period March to April.

SPECIES TULIPS

60

TULIPA TARDA

This delightful, dwarf multi-flowering tulip comes from Central Asia and is one of the smallest of all tulips. Perfect for growing at the edge of a sunny bed or on a rock garden. The grey-green leaves form a rosette around the white, pointed petals with bright yellow centres.

Classification Species tulips.
Colour White with yellow centre.
Height 10cm (4in).
Awards AM H 37 AM W 70.
Flowering period April to May.

  10 cm PERIOD 2-7

TULIPA PRAESTANS 'FUSILIER'

One of a group of multi–flowered tulips which are bright and can have up to six blooms per stem. The flowers are well-shaped and pink streaked yellow in colour.

Classification Species tulips.
Colour Pink streaked yellow.
Height 25cm (10in).
Awards FCC H 42.
Flowering period March to April.

  25 cm PERIOD 1-4

TULIPA KOLPAKOWSKIANA

A dwarf tulip whose flowers are carmine edged yellow in colour. In the same group as the cultivar 'Cynthia', *T. kolpakowskiana* is a multi-flowered variety with twisted, contorted foliage.

Classification Species tulips.
Colour Carmine edged yellow.
Height 15cm (6in).
Flowering period April to May.

15 cm

PERIOD 2-7

TULIPA LINIFOLIA

A very attractive dwarf red tulip which comes from Turkestan. The leaves are slightly glaucous and wavy. The petals are a dull red without and glossy scarlet within.

Classification Species tulips.
Colour Scarlet.
Height 12.5cm (5in).
Awards AM H 32   AM W 70.
Flowering period May.

12.5 cm

PERIOD 5-7

TULIPA BAKERI 'LILAC WONDER'

One of a group of small lilac species.
Considered to be the best of the group,
'Lilac Wonder' is a lilac colour with a
yellow inner centre.

Classification Species tulips.
Colour Lilac with a yellow centre.
Height 15cm (6in).
Year introduced 1971.
Awards FCC H 77.
Flowering period April.

15 cm **PERIOD 2-4**

TULIPA BATALINII

A very small species of tulip with pretty
lemon blooms which presents like a
creamy-yellow version of *T.linifolia* but
with more leaves.

Classification Species tulips.
Colour Lemon.
Height 12.5cm (5in).
Awards FCC W 70 AM H 00.
Flowering period April to May.

12.5 cm **PERIOD 2-7**

Index

Alphabetical listing of botanical names.

INDEX